OLD-FASHIONED CORNERS OF PARIS

Old-fashioned Corners of

PARIS

by Christophe Destournelles

Photographs by Christophe Lefébure

THE LITTLE BOOKROOM · NEW YORK

TABLE OF

CONTENTS

MANUFACTURE DE CHICORÉE
PROTEZ - DELÂTRE
à CAMBRAI (Nord)

Maison fondée en 1809, ne fabriquant que
des produits de QUALITÉ SUPÉRIEURE

PARIS-NEW YORK

ALGER PARIS

MARS-PARIS

Paris à venir

M. F. PARIS

10c

25

Dear S.,

Taking to roads less traveled during my visit, I explored the byways of a Paris I'd previously neglected—probably because visitors don't (or no longer) notice it among the capital's many more familiar avatars: showy Paris, "bourgeois-bohemian" Paris, museum-and-art-gallery Paris, tourist Paris, standardized Paris, Chinese Paris, African Paris, and all the others. As I explored, I found a forgotten Paris that's slightly old-fashioned, provincial, and sometimes endangered—but still surviving and vibrant. You might say an authentic Paris. . . or at least one that's a mine of unexpected experiences and pleasures.

I wandered around from early morning—when I visited bakeries, cafés, and markets—until late at night, when cellar club bands in the Latin Quarter play the kind of jazz you thought you'd only find today in the books of Boris Vian.

I could have told you about my discoveries by text, but I thought it was more appropriate to send you this postcard, which I'm writing in a small café that apparently hasn't changed in thirty years. It reminds me of the bistros in our native Auvergne.

C.

WHAT GOES AROUND...

So which carousel is the capital's oldest? Some say the one in the Luxembourg gardens; others, this one: the Ranelagh carousel, which has been turning since the end of the nineteenth century without the assistance of electricity or a motor. It is powered by the "Carousel Man," who, like Sisyphus with his boulder, labors tirelessly to keep it moving. Generations of happy, watchful children have climbed into the saddle and ridden its battered wooden horses with their patina of age and gentle, fixed gaze.

Watchful? Yes. These children are not just riding, they are competing, too. Clinging to the pole that raises and lowers their horse, the budding riders use sticks to try to spear a ring and win the prize: a free ride. And why not another ride, then one more after that? An entire afternoon spent riding happily through the air...

> *We must be very careful to hold the rod steady and aim it properly. We are coming round. In a few seconds, we will reach the ring. There it is: suspended in the air and swaying gently. It comes nearer. I am getting very close. The time has come. I hold the rod out and aim straight for the center. There! I hear a metallic clink...*

Nathalie Sarraute, *Enfance*, 1983

> *Riding on the carousel of wooden horses, we chased the ring in a last reminder of medieval jousting revived by Walter Scott, where the rider held a metal rod and had to catch a ring suspended above their head as they passed.*

Paul Morand, *Paris*

Luxembourg carousel
Jardin du Luxembourg, 6th arr.

Push carousel
Jardin du Ranelagh, 16th arr.

• **And also:**
Retro carousel
Corner of avenue du Maine and
rue Mouton-Duvernet, 14th arr.

TRUE ZINC

Le Rubis is a timeless café, its counter polished by thousands of elbows and hammered by countless beer glasses, china saucers, and quickly gulped last-ones-for-the-road. The bistro is filled with stories and memories. The surrounding area may have changed radically, becoming increasingly chic, but Le Rubis is the same as it ever was.

Lunch here consists of a rilette sandwich, smoked herring and potatoes dressed in oil, beef Bourguignon, or a selection of cheeses washed down with a glass of Morgon or a beer. There are no stools. Those keen to experience this slice of Parisian life must stand at the counter, rubbing shoulders with construction workers from a neighboring site, local storekeepers who lunch here every day, chattering employees from the office buildings nearby, and wide-eyed tourists. The landlord fetches bottle after bottle of Beaujolais from the reach-in icebox as his cheery wife recommends we try the tart of the day with our coffee. Naturally we order a slice, only too pleased to prolong the pleasure.

Le Rubis
10, rue du Marché-Saint-Honoré, 1st arr.
Tel. 01 42 61 03 34

YESTERDAY ONCE MORE

We thought knitting was for grandmothers. We believed that only weekend fishermen wore hats these days. We saw gloves as something for charitable ladies visiting the sick and poor. How wrong we were!

Today, young women display their taste for handmade clothing and accessories at the tables of stylish cafés, young men sport roguish headwear that adds the final touch to their fashionable look, and both frequent elegant glovers' stores in the Palais-Royal arcades.

The wheel turns. There is nothing new under the Parisian sun... except the endless cycle of fashion and the tradition of deliciously named *magasins de nouveauté.*

Les Parapluies Simon (umbrellas)
56, boulevard Saint-Michel, 6th arr.
Tel. 01 43 54 12 04

**Parapluies Alexandra Sojfer–
Madeleine Gély (umbrellas)**
218, boulevard Saint-Germain, 7th arr.
Tel. 01 42 22 17 02

**Marchand de Bas et Collants
Gérard Durand
(stockings and pantyhose)**
75-77, rue du Bac, 7th arr.
Tel. 01 45 44 98 55

Gants Muriel (gloves)
4, rue des Saussaies, 8th arr.
Tel. 01 42 65 95 34

La Maison du Bouton (buttons)
12, rue de Cotte, 12th arr.
Tel. 01 43 43 95 25

PARIS PISTE

They say a skier was seen racing down the slopes of Montmartre hill early this morning. Sparrows have left spidery tracks on the immaculate blanket that swathes the nearby park. The city is silent, strangely muffled by a visitation that local inhabitants watch for each winter—hopefully, or with a sneaking fear of traffic jams. Snow fell all through the night. Today, the radiant quays are cloaked in white and the sun glints dazzlingly off the River Seine. So put your town shoes away and pull on your snow boots. It is not so cold, but it would be a shame to take a tumble on the sidewalk as you crunch down the street in search of breakfast croissants. The excitement is almost tangible. Parisians rarely have the opportunity to practice winter sports in their hometown. And today is Sunday. Children are hoping the schools will be closed tomorrow. Snow has come to the capital, but it cannot stay for long. They will enjoy it while it lasts.

Strange. Why do snowmen all look the same?

BARBERS AND
THEIR VILLE

As we see in the current crop of advertising, the chic male archetype of the early twenty-first century opts for facial hair. This may take the form of a two- or three-day stubble (possibly more), but it must always be immaculately trimmed. So, slowly but surely, a forgotten trade

is returning to our streets, one we thought was a thing of the past, only of interest to the wealthy or a few eccentrics. Yes, barbers are back and thriving again in certain Parisian salons, which cater to the proud owners of mustaches and beards in need of care. This new generation of barbershops is also popular with those men who are immune to the charms of facial adornment, but keen to experience the unfamiliar sensation of getting a shave. Home shaving is usually dismissed as a chore to be dispatched as summarily as possible, but here, everybody takes his time—anything from twenty minutes to half an hour!

The ritual is much the same in all the shops. The barber prepares the customer's skin with oil before applying shaving cream with a brush. Then comes the shave itself, expertly executed with a straight (aka cutthroat") razor. At this point, the client inevitably visualizes certain

ROJA
BRILLANTINE
"RICINÉE"
LIQUIDE

JAUNE
Topaze

Brillantine
LIQUIDE
du
Dr. HENNA

GRASSE et
PARFUMÉE

LABORATOIRES
D'OEUVRE
LYON

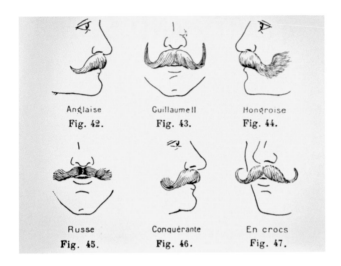

| Anglaise
Fig. 42. | Guillaume II
Fig. 43. | Hongroise
Fig. 44. |
| Russe
Fig. 45. | Conquérante
Fig. 46. | En crocs
Fig. 47. |

sometimes-bloody scenes in westerns or gangster movies... but the moment soon passes as he focuses on the unfamiliar feel of the blade sweeping smoothly over his face. Once the last trace of stubble has vanished, an application of potassium alum soothes the fire kindled on more sensitive skin. Then comes the application of after-shave lotion and/or moisturizing cream, and finally a hot towel draped over the face. A cloud of talcum powder concludes the ceremony.

Every man should try it at least once in his life.

Alain, Maître Barbier-Coiffeur
8, rue Saint-Claude, 3rd arr.
Tel. 01 42 77 55 80

La Barbière de Paris
14, rue Condorcet, 9th arr.
Tel. 01 45 26 92 45

• And also:

Les Mauvais Garçons, 60, rue Oberkampf, 11th arr.

Kiehl's, 13, rue des Martyrs, 9th arr.

Also the hairdressing salons of Little Turkey around
the rue du Faubourg-Saint-Denis, 10th arr.

HEARTS AND SOUL

Like the works of Zola, people either love or hate tripe. Although variety meats are reputed for their subtlety and flavor, they have slowly fallen out of favor, inexorably exiled from household dinner tables and restaurant menus.

Fortunately, the gastronomic renaissance and "indie" cuisine have come to their rescue. There are even restaurants that specialize in these cuts. So much the better! But remember, expert tripe butchers are a rare jewel. Only a handful are to be found in the stores and covered markets of Paris, where they champion variety meats day after day. Anyone keen to find classics of the genre—liver, kidney, tongue, sweetbreads, ear, head, or foot—should visit one of these virtuosi, who can also introduce them to new experiences, such as peck, lamb tripe, honeycomb, fries, spleen, or udder.

Triperie Maurice Vadorin
176, rue Lecourbe, 15th arr.
Tel. 01 48 28 03 32

"" *Then he passed along the sidewalk by the triperie with its calves' feet and heads, the rolled tripe neatly packed in boxes, the brains fastidiously laid in flat baskets, the bloody livers, the purplish kidneys. He paused to inspect long two-wheeled carts covered with a round tarpaulin loaded with halved pigs hung on either side over a bed of straw. Seen from behind, the inside of the cart looked like a tabernacle lit by the rows of naked flesh. On the straw were tin cans catching the dripping blood. Florent was gripped by a fever. The bland smell of the butchers and the pungent smell of the tripe agitated him.* ""*

Émile Zola, *Le Ventre de Paris* (*The Belly of Paris*), 1873, translation by Mark Kurlansky (Modern Library)

THE GARDEN GAMBIT

Whether on a Tuesday afternoon in winter or a Friday lunchtime in August, you will find them there. Calm and focused, they concentrate on the chessboard or lean over the shoulder of a fellow player, looking for the *coup de grâce* that will checkmate their adversary, or eying the timer fixed to the enameled stand.

Like chess enthusiasts all over the world—in New York, Moscow, Budapest, or Belgrade—Parisian players enjoy the tonic scent of greenery and the community spirit of their open-air arena, with its dozen tables and strategically placed benches.

Beginners or masters, young or old, leisurely or quick, they form one of the most remarkable silent shows imaginable, for the benefit of visitors to the Luxembourg gardens. It is a delight to watch them play, while being careful not to disturb their quiet yet terribly expressive games. And why not take the plunge and join them one day? Its equipment supplied by the gardens' owner—the august French Senate—the chess players' circle is a relaxed and genuinely egalitarian society.

Chess games
Jardin du Luxembourg, 6th arr.
Rue Guynemer entrance

33

CARAMEL, BONBONS, AND CHOCOLATE

> ❝ *No sooner had the warm liquid, mixed with the crumbs of the cake, touched my palate than a shudder ran through my whole body, and I stopped, intent on the extraordinary changes that were taking place in me. An exquisite pleasure had invaded my senses, but individual, detached, with no suggestion of its origin. At once the vicissitudes of life had become indifferent to me, its disasters innocuous, its brevity illusory—this new sensation having had on me the effect that love has of filling me with a precious essence; or rather this essence was not in me, it was me.* ❞
>
> Marcel Proust, *Du côté de chez Swann* (*Swann's Way*), 1913 , translation by C. K. Scott Moncrieff (Yale University Press)

To each their madeleine, to each their dream of childhood, and to each their sweet memories of France. For some, these involve Bochard mandarins, Le Roux caramels, Mazet praline chocolates, or Orléans quince preserve. Others will think longingly of macarons from Genot in Nancy, Nevers négus, Lapalisse vérités, Pau coucougnettes, or Bourges forestines. . .

34

These delights and other crisp, melting, sharp, rounded, or sensual pleasures are to be found in traditional confectionery stores—sugar-scented temples of temptation where visitors put aside their resolutions and forget the passing of time as they immerse themselves in sheer bliss. Among these stores are À l'Étoile d'Or in Pigalle, with its high priestess, the legendary Denise Acabo; À la Mère de Famille in rue du Faubourg-Montmartre; and the more understated Tétrel in Palais-Royal. Gleaming jars, antique wood counters and shelves, and wrapping paper from another age—there are so many reasons to explore these Candy Lands, with their continents of fondant chocolate and islands of fruit. Travel there alone or in convivial company...

Tétrel
44, rue des Petits-Champs, 2nd arr.
Tel. 01 42 96 59 58

À la Mère de Famille
35, rue du Faubourg-Montmartre, 9th arr.
Tel. 01 47 70 83 69

Chez Denise Acabo–À l'Étoile d'Or
30, rue Pierre-Fontaine, 9th arr.
Tel. 01 48 74 59 55

• And also:

Legrand Filles et Fils
1, rue de la Banque, 2nd arr.
Tel. 01 42 60 07 12

BALLADS
AND BELLY LAUGHS

Just for once, we will pass on the stand-up comedy of a rising young comedian, take a rain check on the one-woman show performed by an impending star, and instead choose a musical performance (*Ne me twitte pas, La France d'en bas tombe de haut, or Hollande met le P.I. Bas*) with its allusions to the faults of French leaders, gloom seasoned with a zest of cynical irony, and barrack-room comedy lampooning the dysfunctions of the political world. Here, the headlines are dissected by obviously anticlerical troublemakers with, and this is crucial, a wonderful mastery of the French language. If you are not averse to mingling with the regular crowd, not generally young or particularly stylish, try the Caveau de la République or the Théâtre des Deux Ânes, two supremely Parisian—and supremely bawdy—institutions.

Inspired by the Société du Caveau founded in 1729, the Caveau de la République opened in 1901 in the very aptly named Ferme de la Vacherie (Jibe Farm). It has hosted many legendary, very French comedians over the years, including Les Frères Ennemis and, more recently, Laurent Ruquier and Gaspard Proust at the start of their careers. Show posters

illustrated by great cartoonists such as Gab, Cabu, and Siné are very much part of the theater's history.

Around since 1920, the second theater (successively named La Truie qui file, L'Araignée, Le Porc-Épic, and La Taverne des Truands, before finally opting for Les Deux Ânes) is a noble avatar of yesterday's Montmartre cabarets. It has a maxim: "Bray and laugh." Here, Régis Mailhot, Albert Algoud, Isabelle Alonso, and Bernard Mabille—to mention only the youngest—perpetuate the art of the press review. The jokes are occasionally heavy-handed, often astute, and... so very French! Some would say Rabelaisian and even a little too much for visitors from less ribald cultures.

Caveau de la République 1, boulevard Saint-Martin, 3rd arr. Tel. 01 42 78 44 45	**Théâtre des Deux Ânes** 100, boulevard de Clichy, 18th arr. Tel. 01 46 06 10 26

THAT FLOATING FEELING

oating. Both the word and the pastime conjure up another age when the Impressionists acquired a taste for excursions on the Seine or Marne rivers. These outings were immortalized in the paintings of Monet, Renoir, and Caillebotte, and the literature of Zola and Maupassant.

Boating on Lac Daumesnil began later, at the start of the twentieth century. This 30-acre stretch of water is the largest lake in the Bois de Vincennes, encircling two islands linked by a bridge. The island of Reuilly is by far the favorite, with its romantic cave and rotunda built by iconic Second Empire architect Gabriel Davioud.

When the sun shines, freshwater *matelots* savor the unique pleasures of boating on the tranquil waters, each at their own pace. The best prepared have brought a hamper to picnic in their boat or on the grass of the banks in the shade of an oak or weeping willow. To fully enter into the aquatic spirit, we recommend traditional costume: a striped sailor's jersey (made in France) and, obviously, the flat, narrow-brimmed straw boater affected by the earliest aficionados.

Lac Daumesnil	**Lac des Minimes**	**Bois de Boulogne**
Route de Ceinture (Beltway)	Route de Nogent, beside the Chalet	Northern end of Lac Inférieur,
Lac Daumesnil, 12th arr.	de la Porte Jaune, 12th arr.	16th arr.
Tel. 01 43 28 19 20	Tel. 06 86 08 01 12	

NIGHTRIDERS

Should I bet on 5 to place or win in the third?
Unless I try a combination with 3...

There is horse racing at Vincennes tonight. The *hippodrome* draws huge crowds for prestige races such as the Grand Prix d'Amérique, but it is much quieter this evening. The air is a little chilly, but there are other reasons for the declining popularity of racetracks, especially at night. The Internet and specialized TV channels are mainly to blame, since people bet at home rather than traveling to the track by subway or car.

Consequently, on evenings like this, there are only a few diehards clutching racing journals (*Tiercé Magazine* or *France Turf*), and the occasional group of friends who come to dine at one of the restaurants. They look cheerful. Racetracks are fine places to visit after dark, especially when the horses and their jockeys gallop down the cinder track in the glow of the floodlights.

Remember to place a bet. Nothing outrageous, of course, just a little fun. Winning means taking a gamble!

Hippodrome de Vincennes
2, route de la Ferme, 12th arr.
Tel. 01 49 77 14 70

BOIS
CHARBONS
PRIMAGAZ

OUVERT

ATTENTION À
LA MARCHE

WINES AND COAL

I n the nineteenth century, many people from France's central Auvergne region moved to Paris. Initially, most worked as water carriers, a trade that went into decline during the Second Empire period as water mains spread their roots under the capital. Then, these natives of the Massif Central mountains began to trade in wood (and charcoal) and opened cafés. The more enterprising combined the two. Bars kept by these *bougnats* appeared everywhere, identifiable from their trademark "Wines and Coal" sign. Later, as the demand for wood and coal steadily fell, the most ambitious *bougnats* began to serve food and rent out rooms.

The last true "Wines and Coal" café closed a few years back. It was in the eleventh arrondissement of Paris. However, between the Jardin des Plantes and rue Mouffetard, you can still see a historic *bougnat* founded in 1840. It sells all kinds of fuel, including wood and coal. Sadly, there is no bar where regulars can while away the time over a glass of Saint-Pourçain.

Marcillac Combustibles
9, rue du Puits-de l'Ermite, 5th arr.
Tel. 01 47 07 92 27

A FLOWER FOR
ÉMILE FAGUET

"I doubt there will be any flowers left on Faguet's grave in Père Lachaise cemetery, although he certainly had a greater feeling for literary art than poor Jim Morrison."

A touch provocatively, Simon Liberati wrote these words in one of his 113 studies of romantic literature (Flammarion, 2013). The late *homme de lettres* he is referring to is none other than Émile Faguet (1847–1916), member of the Académie Française and the author of many books on politics and teaching, and especially literary essays that long featured prominently on student reading lists. Today, he is entirely forgotten. Even Liberati mistakenly directs the curious to Père Lachaise, when Faguet is actually buried in the tenth division of the Montparnasse cemetery.

But there remains the poignant, appealing idea of setting out to explore these names that are engraved in stone, but not in our memories. The cemeteries of Montmartre, Montparnasse, Père-Lachaise, and Passy hold the remains of thousands of men and women who achieved a certain fame—or even glory—in their lifetimes, but are now consigned to eternal solitude and oblivion.

So let us leave flowers on the grave of Émile Faguet. . . and possibly visit the quays of the Seine to find one of his works in the stall of a *bouquiniste* there.

RETRO RESURRECTION

The throwaway consumer philosophy that emerged in the Sixties is now starting to get a little old. The new trend is to repair, restore, and renovate. And nothing can compare to the skills of certain artisans hidden away in their little workshops, gifted surgeons who operate on gutted mattresses, stripped chairs, stopped clocks, defunct shavers, silent transistor radios, and geriatric record players. Armed with patience, ingenuity, determination, experience, and skill, they put horsehair back into seats, drip oil onto gears, and apply leather to worn bindings. They adeptly restore that Seventies couch found in a flea market, reawaken vintage vacuum-tube radios, and generally revive objects which often have a fascinating history.

From the courtyards of the faubourg Saint-Antoine to the engagingly old-fashioned stores of the sixth arrondissement, explore the world of these remarkable craftspersons.

Hubert François - Clockmaker
43, rue Madame, 6th arr.
Tel. 01 45 44 22 00

**Paléophonies–vintage transistor,
radio, and gramophone repair**
16, rue de Vaugirard, 6th arr.
Tel. 01 46 33 20 17

Electric Shaver Clinic
42, rue de la Roquette, 11th arr.
Tel. 01 47 00 12 70

**Spécial Literie—
mattress renovation and chair caning**
19, rue de Cotte, 12th arr.
Tel. 01 43 43 61 7

CROSS MY PALM

Tarot fortune-telling," explains Pascal Altiz, "doesn't work miracles. It can provide guidance in certain situations, give advice, and point to the right and wrong times to do different things."

In the Fifties, there was a fortune-teller's trailer in each district of Paris. Now just two remain in the entire city.

For decades, the older trailer has been occupied by the mysterious Madame Ranah, protected by the mighty Lion of Belfort statue, the king of place Denfert-Rochereau. The other, which attracts visitors to Père-Lachaise cemetery and other passers-by with its vivid images of colorful, poetic tarot cards, belongs to Pascal Altiz, "Messenger of the Tarot and Magus of French carnival workers."

These two temples of urban arcana offer private sessions complete with a plethora of tarot cards, pendulums, and perfumed candles from morning to evening, answering the questions of star-crossed lovers and anxious employees.

Magus Altiz, heir to a long line of street fortune-tellers, is at home in the modern world. The great-grandson of a medium who found fame in France after traveling the globe, he inherited his clairvoyant gifts from his grandmother. When you knock on his door, remember the wise words of Sâr Rabindranath Duval, performed by the great French comedian Pierre Dac: "our future lies ahead. . . but we just have to turn around and it's behind us."

Magus Altiz's trailer	**Madam Ranah's trailer**
Opposite 61, boulevard de Ménilmontant, 11th arr.	Opposite the rue Froidevaux métro exit
Tel. 06 03 99 10 1	Place Denfert-Rochereau, 14th arr.

Mme RANAH

Chiromancie

Tarologie

Le doute fait souffrir
La certitude tranquilise l'esprit

Reçoit tous les jours sauf dimanche

FAMILY FLOTILLAS

> *I live just around the corner from the Luxembourg Gardens, where I spend all my time. I write there, and play with the children, help them sail their boats, etc. There is an old bent man who sails a toy boat on the pool, with the most beautiful rapt face you ever saw. When I am old enough to no longer have to make excuses for not working, I shall have a weathered derby hat like his and spend my days sailing a toy boat in the Luxembourg Gardens.*
>
> *A Faulkner Chronology* by Michel Gresset (University Press of Mississippi) quoting from *Selected Letters of William Faulkner,* Joseph Blotner, ed. (Random House, 1966)

There are few places where pleasure boats, barges, submarines, speedboats, schooners, and other, sometimes whimsical, vessels can be seen on the same stretch of water. Not to mention the local ducks come to enjoy the show and the cluster of immobile cherubs posing for eternity in the center of the pond. For over a century, the public has been enjoying the never-ending nautical maneuvers on the pond in Luxembourg Gardens, admission free.

Visitors can bring their own boat—lovingly maintained and handed down by a grandfather or awarded in recognition of some scholastic achievement—or hire one of the attractive yachts available there. Some date back to 1922, the year when the Paudeau family (originally from the Vendée region) took over the boat hire concession and put together a flotilla of miniature craft, each of them different.

Model boats in the Tuileries gardens	**Model boats in the Luxembourg gardens**
Jardin des Tuileries, 1st arr.	Jardin du Luxembourg, 6th arr.
On the pond near the Carrousel	On the central pond

64

CULINARY CRAFTS

S tores "of the mouth"—a rather old-fashioned, typically French expression that handily encompasses bakers, confectioners, deli owners, butchers, purveyors of offal and poultry, fishmongers, cheesemongers, greengrocers, and wine merchants. Do Parisians appreciate just how fortunate they are to still have so many gourmet emporia just around the corner, while others must drive to the mall to restock their pantries and refrigerators? Any self-respecting *Homo parisianus* should cherish "their" butcher who plies them with salt-meadow lamb cutlets, veal escalopes from calves raised on their mother's milk, or ham stewed on the bone in its stock. They should prize the deli owner who faithfully prepares homemade headcheese with parsley, chitterlings sausages with Charroux mustard, and grated carrots lightly pickled in vinaigrette. And they should sing the praises of the cheesemonger by whose grace they can savor the delights of Laqueuille blue, marbled Aravis, and Cajassous from the Cévennes without taking to the road.

PASTIS, PINBALL, AND POKER

They are faceless, anonymous, forgotten places. Bars you can pass a hundred times without a second glance... until, for some reason or another, you decide to step through the door. Inside, surrounded by familiar noises, scents, knickknacks, and details, you come to the conclusion that this café has not changed a jot over the last twenty, thirty, or fifty years. The vintage Ricard ashtray, unsullied by cigarette butts for years, is still in its place—who can tell what the future will bring? Endless, serried ranks of bottles parade behind the counter, displaying their litany of distinctly French names: Noilly Prat, Byrrh, Dubonnet, Bartissol... The walls are decorated with ancient, darkly nostalgic photographs of cities and provincial scenes, often from the Auvergne; the tables are Formica; the chairs wooden.

The coffee is never anything to write home about and a demi of Amstel beer is never very expensive. A pinball machine glows in its corner, there is sometimes a billiard table in the back room for competitive customers, and, in compliance with an unwritten law, the barkeep has dice and a deck of cards ready behind the counter. Regulars quietly sip their Casanis pastis, students flirt noisily or study in silence, and solitary diners chow down on a croque-monsieur or an omelet as they read their newspaper. The world continues to turn...

Au Petit Bar	**Le Carrefour**
7, rue du Mont-Thabor, 1st arr.	2, rue Monsieur-le-Prince, 6th arr
Tel. 01 42 36 62 09	

SWINGING PARIS

Have we always been swingers? Depictions of swings feature on Ancient Greek vases dating back 2,800 years! The type of swinger has changed, though. Once an adult pastime, swings are now a children's plaything. In Parc Monceau, for instance, tiny tots are cautiously propelled by their wary parents in a swaying motion scarcely more violent than the rocking of a cradle, while their older siblings heave with all their might, dreaming of looping the loop.

Seeing their intent faces, we find ourselves lost in our own childhood memories: the feeling of freedom and sense of taking flight, thumbing our noses at the law of gravity; the giddiness of overcoming our fears and reveling in the breathtaking rush.

The swings in Paris parks are the old-fashioned kind: two-seated and built of splinter-free metal, each in its own little enclosure. They are charming rides whose only failing is that they do not come free.

Traditional swings	
Jardin du Luxembourg, 6th arr.	Square Marigny, 8th arr.
Champ-de-Mars, 7th arr.	Parc Montsouris, 13th arr.
Parc Monceau, 8th arr.	Square des Batignolles, 17th arr.
	Parc des Buttes-Chaumont, 19th arr.

BOTANICAL NOSTRUMS

H erbalism was a recognized trade from the 14th century on, until Marshal Pétain banned it in 1941. After that, pharmacists were the only authorized purveyors of medicinal plants. In theory, all the herbalists' stores in France should have closed. Yet a handful remained, including the one in rue d'Amsterdam, Paris.

Its antique storefront suggests how little it has changed since it opened in 1880. That impression is confirmed when you step through the portal. A powerful scent of dried herbs fills the air and the eye is immediately drawn to the fine wooden furnishings and shelves, holding hundreds of varieties of plants in white paper packets, along with flasks of extracts and essential oils. On the counters or in glazed cabinets stand ranks of glass and ceramic jars. Antique scales rub shoulders with wicker baskets.

But this is no quaint museum. While curious passers-by and tourists may drop in to taste the unique atmosphere of this phytotherapeutic emporium, they are heavily outnumbered by the regular customers in search of dried herbs and flowers, in bulk or already packaged to go.

Herboristerie de la place Clichy
87, rue d'Amsterdam, 8th arr.
Tel. 01 48 74 83 32

BOOTHWATCH

> *—Hello, operator? I'd like to place a call.*
> *—What number?*
> *—I want to speak to Asnières 22...*
>
> Fernand Raynaud's famous *Le 22 à Asnières* sketch

If he were given a glimpse of the present, Fernand Raynaud would certainly have been astonished by the sight of crowds with their eyes or ears constantly glued to their cell phones, everywhere from the subway to movie theaters and restaurants.

But of course Parisians in the year 2031 will be equally shocked to learn that their fellow citizens once had to stand in line at a counter to make a call. And to hear that the installation of thousands of telephone booths in the capital was once seen as a great leap forward will be bound to raise an eyebrow or two.

Today, phone booths are a dying breed, removed for reasons of cost and obsolescence. Many have vanished since the turn of the century and experts predict that only two will remain in each district of Paris in the very near future.

So why not try one out while you still can? They are ugly, dirty, and all too often vandalized or even out of order. Does it matter? If you look carefully—especially around rail stations—you can still find vintage coin-operated models. Prepare your change and journey back in time...

PHILATELY AT MARIGNY

Just a few decades ago, stamp collecting was a virtually essential rite of passage for boys. Fathers passed on their postal treasures to their sons. Grandmothers put aside envelopes with attractive or unusual stamps for their grandchildren. Kids bought large albums, carefully sorted their finds, and used stamp-hinges to attach them to the pages. For most, the hobby lasted a few weeks, months, or even years; but for a few, philately remained a lifelong passion.

Stamps are not terribly popular today. First, because we do not use so many. Mainly, they have been replaced by anonymous printed stickers. Second, because we are sending fewer letters, preferring to call, text, or email. Even the value of collector stamps has suffered since the rise of the Internet and the breakup of the market.

So it is surprising to find a stamp market still trading at the junction of avenue de Marigny and avenue Gabriel, a remnant of the fashion (or even craze) for philately that swept Paris after the issue of the first French postage stamp in 1849. Trading fairs subsequently sprang up here and there, in the Palais-Royal and Luxembourg gardens, for instance. Stores

opened near the Bourse (especially in the passage des Panoramas) and around the Hôtel Drouot auction rooms, where many remain today.

The stamp market on the Champs-Élysées owes its existence to a rich collector. At the end of the 19th century, he bequeathed a lot, the Carré Marigny, to the City of Paris, with the proviso that an open-air stamp market should be allowed to use it. Busier on some days than others, the Carré is home to an amicable community of professional traders and hobbyists who display their wares on benches. Along with collectors, the market attracts tourists... and movie buffs, who imagine catching sight of Audrey Hepburn and Cary Grant there as they visualize the famous scene from the Stanley Donen picture *Charade*.

Stamp Market
At the corner of avenue de Marigny and
avenue Gabriel, 8th arr.
Thursday, Saturday, Sunday and holidays

• And also:
Philately stores at the start of rue La Fayette, 9th arr.

TAKING A SHINE TO PARIS

I t is odd. We are tempted to believe that shoe-shiners are part of Parisian history—street traders who once haunted the capital's squares and sidewalks, but can now only be seen on vintage black-and-white postcards. Yet when we search for evidence of this imagined past, we realize it is hard to find. There are few or no photographs and very little or nothing to be found in books or movies. It seems that Paris had virtually no shoe-shiners, so common in other Western countries where they wielded the tools of their trade to bring a mirror-like sheen to the footwear of well-heeled gentlemen.

Yet, paradoxically, there are now a few stores offering this service to those who can afford to take a short break from their daily routine. Brushing, waxing, and polishing are not to be hurried or taken lightly. They demand skill, technique, accessories, and carefully-chosen products. The ritual unfolds in the company of enthusiasts and in convivial surroundings that put the visitor at ease, making the experience all the more enjoyable.

Salon Baba	**Talon Rouge**
34, rue Jean-Mermoz, 8th arr.	10, rue du Laos, 15th arr.
Tel. 01 42 56 35 53	Tel. 09 51 93 27 91

PHOTO BOOTH FOLLIES

Were you aware that Andy Warhol installed a photo booth at the Factory to take shots of visiting celebrities and less eminent callers, some of which he then used in his legendary screen-printed creations? The idea came to him one day in the company of art collector Ethel Scull, when she had her photo taken in the booth on the corner of Broadway and 52nd Street. The snapshot formed the raw material for his famous *Ethel Scull 36 Times*, one of his first successes.

And it was actually in New York that the first "automated photo studio" or Photomaton was introduced in 1926. Invented by an American of Russian extraction, Anatol Josepho, it proved an immediate hit with both the general public and artists. As soon as the innovation reached France in the late Twenties, the Surrealists became great Photomaton fans.

However, the magic of these unpredictable automatons faded with the arrival of digital technology, which provided four identical, crushingly flawless snapshots in a square instead of strip format.

Fortunately, over the last few years, a few traditional booths of the kind still found in Paris in the Seventies and Eighties have reappeared here and there, often imported from Eastern Europe. They remind us of those

far-off days as we close the drape, turn the stool to adjust its height, and bob around until our face is firmly in the center of the mirror window. We then slot a coin into the belly of the machine and hold our breath, waiting for the warning light and subsequent flash. A few seconds later comes another. Four explosions of light, four poses, four different photos. We step out of the booth and wait as long as it takes for the machinery to spit out our strip of paper. Even then, we have to remain patient while it dries before we can at last retrieve it with care and admire the results.

A faintly grainy, slightly coarse black-and-white picture taken in an unflattering light that vaguely distorts our features. . . Yes, that's us! That's really us!

Bonton Photomaton
5, boulevard des Filles-du-Calvaire, 3rd arr.

Maison Rouge Photomaton
10, boulevard de la Bastille, 12th arr.

Citadium Photomaton
50-56, rue Caumartin, 9th arr.

Palais de Tokyo Photomaton
13, avenue du Président-Wilson, 16th arr.

• And also:
Cabines Harcourt du MK2 Bibliothèque
128-162, avenue de France, 13th arr.

THE LAST VESPASIENNE

Among the revolutions that have changed the face of Paris, few recall the one at the very start of the Eighties that swept away an important piece of street furniture: the *vespasienne*, less elegantly known as the *pissoir*. The *vespasienne* initially appeared in the first half of the 19th century. Different types were designed until Gabriel Davioud came up with the model that would remain familiar for more than a century: a cast-iron structure painted green, with Corinthian pillars, a small roof, and two half-moon screens. By the 1930s, more than 1,200 had invaded the French capital.

Vespasiennes were free to use, but also had their drawbacks. They were for men only and smelled less than fragrant. Their critics also claimed they were breeding grounds for various diseases and hotbeds of illegal trafficking and unmentionable sexual practices.

They did indeed provide suitable shelter for covert encounters, an advantage that led Second World War Resistance workers to meet in them.

Today, Decaux automatic public toilets have replaced M. Davioud's *vespasiennes*.

Only one has escaped the purge and nobody knows why. . . or for how long. Covered in tags and stickers of every kind, the last *vespasienne* stands on boulevard Arago, in front of the long, featureless wall of the Santé prison. Cabs, ambulances, and police trucks stop there, their occupants aware that a place where you can satisfy a pressing need free of charge is well worth knowing.

Vespasienne
Opposite 86, boulevard Arago, 14th arr.

THE PIPES, THE PIPES ARE CALLING...

The pipe smoker's ritual is an act of resistance, defying modern social injunctions and the stresses of urban life. Tamping tobacco down into the bowl of a pipe one small pinch at a time and then lighting, smoking, dismantling, and cleaning it are all stages in a ceremony that demand specialized paraphernalia: a tobacco pouch, a tamper and pipe-cleaners, and even a pipe-stand for the most devoted aficionados. Not to mention a carefully chosen brand of tobacco.

And the pipe itself? While diehard smokers have their own favorite addresses, lovers of curiosities and antique stores flock to the arcades of Palais-Royal. À l'Oriental has been supplying cigarette holders, tobacco pots, and meerschaum and other pipes—new and old (but not chewed!)—for more than half a century. It is also a monument to the glory of exotic brands: Don Carlos, Chacom, Butz-Choquin, Savinelli, Peterson, Ser Jacopo, L'Anatra, Viprati, Ashton, RVK, Becker, Musicò, Castello, Charles Cassetari, G. Georges, and others.

A far cry from the world of synthetic apple-flavored e-cigarettes!

À l'Oriental
Palais-Royal Gardens
22, galerie de Chartres, 1st arr.
Tel. 01 42 96 43 16

SUBTERRANEAN JAZZ

The rue de la Huchette is a street with a vocation: to protect the heritage of the Latin Quarter. Ionesco's play *La Cantatrice chauve* (The Bald Soprano) has been performed here almost every evening for more than fifty years without a break, and movie buffs have been miming the lewd gestures of *The Rocky Horror Picture Show*'s sweet transvestites for decades. These theatrical phenomena aside, behind the street's kebab shops and touristy onion-soup restaurants beats the vibrant heart of the Paris jazz scene. At the Caveau de la Huchette, dancers of swing and be-bop (and lindy-hop modernists) meet almost conspiratorially to party blissfully through the night. On the tiny stage, musicians play Duke Ellington and Glenn Miller, and cover classics

by the Andrews Sisters. At times, you could almost believe you are hearing the trumpet riffs of the great Boris Vian, a late lamented regular, rising to the stone vault.

The world-famous Caveau has hosted some of the greatest names in jazz, from Claude Bolling to Sidney Bechet, Memphis Slim or Sacha Distel. It is still a temple of music, but also one that is now dedicated to Terpsichore, thanks to the work of the Rats de Cave school, which teaches enthusiasts to master the passes and hops of jazz dance.

The house asks little of its guests—just to stamp their feet, clap their hands, swing, dance, and sing!

Caveau de la Huchette
5, rue de la Huchette, 5th arr.
Tel. 01 43 26 65 05

LODGINGS OF PARIS

Th

These establishments are a million miles from the boutique hotels of the capital and their meticulously contrived ambiences. If a comparison were needed, we should look to two-star establishments in the Lot-et-Garonne district, forgotten inns standing opposite a sub-prefecture on a provincial square, or family-run digs for distressed traveling salespeople. They are definitely not something you would expect to find in Paris, these few remaining survivors from days when people booked into a hotel to sleep soundly after a long day on the road selling door to door. Some are located in smart neighborhoods (place Dauphine or the heart of Saint-Germain-des-Prés) and still sport traditional homey curtains and waxed tablecloths, refugees from an age now totally alien to anyone under twenty. What a journey back in time! A whiff of nostalgia for those bold souls who venture inside and are handed a key from the board behind the ancient reception desk. Whether you are staying for a single night or starting a new life far from prying eyes, these havens of peace live up to their warm promise.

Hôtel Henri-IV	**Hôtel Jean-Bart**
25, place Dauphine, 1st arr.	9, rue Jean-Bart, 6th arr.
Tel. 01 43 54 44 53	Tel. 01 45 48 29 13

RIVERSIDE READING

When a character in a Patrick Modiano novel mentions a book "found on the quays," the expression conjures up memories of a different world. The quays in question are obviously those on the banks of the Seine, where antique and second-hand booksellers know as *bouquinistes* ply their trade. Their places of business have been there since the 16th century and are listed as World Heritage sites by Unesco. They form an integral part of the Parisian landscape. Theoretically, each *bouquiniste* has four lockers two meters wide and painted "wagon green," which turn into stalls when opened. There are about 250 *bouquinistes* on the Right Bank between pont Marie and quai du Louvre, and on the Left Bank between quai de la Tournelle and quai Voltaire. Their three kilometers of open-air bookstore boast nearly 500,000 volumes—not to mention engravings, journals and magazines, postcards, and knickknacks for tourists.

If you take the time to browse through these hundreds of green boxes, you realize their treasures are not only of interest to elderly gentlemen who collect dusty, yellowing tomes. All kinds of customers can be attracted by a name, title, or cover; listen to the *bouquiniste*'s advice. . . and finally return home with a book "found on the quays." They will never forget where they bought that book, in the shadow of Notre-Dame Cathedral or the Conciergerie.

Right-Bank *bouquinistes*	**Left-Bank *bouqinistes***
From pont Marie to quai du Louvre	From quai de la Tournelle to quai Voltaire

BRIC-A-BROC

In a famous article published in the *Mercure de France* journal in June 1913, Georges Duhamel compared Guillaume Apollinaire's collection of poetry *Alcools* to a second-hand store.

"I say 'second-hand store' because so many disparate objects have ended up in this junk shop, some of them of value, but none the fruit of the trader's own work. Of course, that is one of the characteristics of the second-hand store: it resells, but does not manufacture. It sometimes holds curiosities; in its grimy displays, you may find a precious gem among the trash. Everything here has come from other places, but the gem is pleasant to admire. As for the rest, it is a collection of fake paintings, patched exotic clothing, bicycle accessories, and personal hygiene implements. Fractious, confusing miscellany replaces art in this cluster of items."

There are few traditional second-hand stores left in Paris. Gone are the mysterious bazaars with their clutter of worthless articles and occasional treasures, presided over by fascinating characters. Even the Saint-Ouen flea market has lost this magic. Today, the joys of rummaging through bric-à-brac for discarded items and remnants of bygone days are only to be tasted in the open air. Early in the morning at the Vanves flea market or a little later at the Aligre market, regulars wait for the arrival of certain house-clearance specialists. As the goods are unloaded, they hunt through the cardboard boxes, old suitcases, and even garbage can liners. They argue over some finds with other rummagers, negotiate and trade. And sometimes, they come across a rare jewel: a book signed by one of their literary idols and miraculously saved from destruction at the hands of uncaring heirs, or an antique Chinese vase mistaken for a cheap copy.

Marché d'Aligre	**Puces de Vanves**
Place d'Aligre, 12th arr.	Avenue Georges-Lafenestre
Every day except Monday	and avenue Marc-Sangnier, 14th arr.
8 am to 1:30 pm	Every weekend from 8 am to 1 pm

BELLE ÉPOQUE BISTRO

Chartier could be the last restaurant in Paris that can properly be termed a *bouillon*, since the house soup is back on its winter menu at the unbeatable price of 1 euro! Originally, that was what a *bouillon* was: a restaurant serving a very cheap beef broth. *Bouillons* were the brainchild of Mr. Duval, a butcher by trade, who opened the first eatery of this kind in the 1860s. It was mainly frequented by workers from the wholesale food market, Les Halles. Later, the Chartier brothers copied the concept, launching a number of bistros including Chartier, Bouillon Racine, Vagenende, and Bistrot de la Gare.

The Chartier establishment, which opened in rue du Faubourg-Montmartre in 1896, has retained its fin de siècle panache. Everywhere is woodwork, brass, tile, and mirrors. The drawers where regulars used to leave their napkins are still there and the formidably efficient waiters continue to wear vests and white aprons. Glasses clink, cutlery chinks, and the dining hall echoes to the chatter of tourists and Parisians, delighted by this period setting where they can enjoy a timeless French cuisine that revolves around egg mayonnaise, smoked herring with potatoes in oil, calf's head, coq au vin, baba au rhum, and chocolate mousse. Even the prices seem to be a century old... or almost!

Following an ancient, ageless tradition, the waiter scribbles the check on a napkin. It would be worth coming back just for that!

Bouillon Chartier
7, rue du Faubourg-Montmartre, 9th arr.
Tel. 01 47 70 86 29

VINTAGE MOVIE MANIA

Where else than Paris—and more specifically the Latin Quarter—can you decide to see an old movie in a darkened theater on the spur of the moment and have such a wide choice?

Today, Laurence Olivier's *Hamlet* is being shown at the Champo. Just next door, the Filmothèque is screening Jean-Paul Le Chanois's 1958 version of *Les Misérables*, starring Jean Gabin. You want something more lighthearted? How about William Wyler's *Roman Holiday* at Le Reflet Médicis, featuring Audrey Hepburn on her scooter and Gregory Peck. Or, on reflection, why not a Hitchcock? There is one on the bill at the Desperado (formerly the Action-Écoles), also showing a movie directed by Jean-Pierre Mocky, owner of the theater. And if you feel like a stroll first, there is a festival of Westerns in full swing at the Action Christine.

The neighborhood has been through endless changes—and even upheavals—over the last few decades. So has the way we watch movies—more than ever in our homes, downloaded from the Internet. Even so, the theaters in the Latin Quarter are still holding out against everything modern technology can throw at them, surfing on a wave of movie mania that began after World War II in 1948, when Éric Rohmer began to host the Latin Quarter Ciné-Club in rue Danton, attended by Rivette, Godard, Chabrol, and Truffaut among others.

CINEMA

LE CHAMPO

048381

STUDIO CHRISTINE 2
PARIS

ENTRÉE

PLAY THE TOURIST

P lace du Tertre? The mere mention of the name is usually enough to make the average Parisian grimace in disgust before embarking on a disdainful, inevitably over-the-top critique of the hordes of baseball cap-wearing, snap-happy tourists shepherded by a guide with an umbrella, shoddy souvenir stores, tacky artists, and overpriced, mediocre restaurants.

But probe further and you will usually learn that the Parisian in question has never actually set foot in place du Tertre. Their scorn is based on vague recollections of TV reports and 1950s American movies with an accordion soundtrack.

Yet the place du Tertre quarter has many faces, some of them obscure. When it is free of "intruders" early in the morning or late at night, it seems disconcerting, confusing, stripped bare. The curious may even glimpse ghosts from Montmartre's past.

And during the day? Obviously, there are tourists, crowds of tourists, lured by the legend of the area and its quaint artists' square. But those who are ready to suspend judgment and watch the portraitists at work find themselves opening up to the picturesque, good-natured ambience and, like everyone else, enjoying the serious or amused expressions of the models as their traits are consigned to paper, portrayed with precision or a certain artistic license. Why not try it? You can pose alone, in pairs, in groups of three or four, or even with a pet. It is up to you. Talk to the artists and hear their odd tales. Smile at the rubbernecks and leave with your portrait or caricature rolled up under your arm. And with a different view of place du Tertre. . .

Portraitists and caricaturists
Place du Tertre, 18th arr.

THE TOWN CRIER

New York Herald Tribune! *New York Herald Tribune*! How we wish the itinerant vendor were a pretty, short-haired blonde touting for customers with a strong American accent. But this is no movie and we are not hearing Jean Seberg play Patricia in Godard's *Breathless*.

Parisian streets no longer echo to the cries of street newspaper vendors. . . except in Saint-Germain-des-Prés, where Ali Akbar has trodden the paving stones for more than thirty-five years with his copies of *Le Monde* under one arm. Saint-Germain-des-Prés has changed radically during that time, but Ali still brings a smile to the faces of customers sitting at tables outside the celebrated Les Deux Magots café as he regales them with fanciful stories and chats to all and sundry passers-by or visitors to the area.

PILI: A BRIGHT IDEA

Every Parisian child has played with the oversize, magical map with its string of telltale lights guiding passengers through the labyrinthine Métro.

Pili, the acronym of Plan indicateur lumineux d'itinéraires ("light indicator itinerary map"), began to provide directions for Métro users in 1937. It was an immediate hit. By the Eighties, there were 124 Pili maps all over the capital.

Sadly, their increasingly frequent breakdowns and dated design, the opening of Line 14, and the emergence of new technologies (including cell phone apps) inevitably led to their retirement.

One Pili map after another quietly vanished over the years, generally unmourned. However, a few specimens remain, including one in the Palais-Royal-du-Musée-du-Louvre station, where the curious can press the button that corresponds to their destination and see the shortest route light up.

Even when the last Pili has vanished, we will still be able to admire P.I.L.I., an installation by artist Philippe Favier on display in Pyramides station, inspired by poet Jacques Roubaud... and the Pili, of course!

BRING YOUR NAPKIN RING

> *" The starter?*
> *Egg mayonnaise for the gentleman?*
> *Grated carrots for the lady?*
> *And to drink? Red wine? Is a pitcher OK?*
> *Straight away, Monsieur Christophe!*
> *Egg mayonnaise and carrots for table 8!*
> *And don't forget your napkins in the locker.*
> *They're not going to come to your table on their own! "*

Le Pied de Fouet is the kind of local restaurant that those in the know tend not to advertise. The strategically positioned napkin cabinet makes it clear what sort of place this is: the kind of eatery everyone would like to have as a neighbor. Generally smart, the customers of every age are undeterred by the plain simplicity of the establishment, a former stagecoach inn, and gossip cheerfully as they enjoy its home-cooked dishes (including sautéed chicken livers, entrecôte with hand-mashed potatoes, and skate with capers).

The menu changes every day. Customers should not expect to linger over their lunch or dinner. The house policy is rapid customer turnover—good for business!

Au Pied de Fouet
45, rue de Babylone, 7th arr.
Tel. 01 47 05 12 27

PACKING A PUNCH

Children today have plenty of hi-tech gadgets to entertain them: Wii and PlayStation consoles, iPads, and so on. Even so, would they pass on the chance to see a real Punch & Judy show of the kind still performed in certain Paris parks?

Our little cherubs laugh at each blow of the nightstick, giggle at the ludicrous pomposity of the *gendarme* (the very model of blinkered authority), enjoy the cantankerousness of Madelon, wife of Guignol (the French name for Punch), and fall about as they watch the drunken antics of his good

friend Gnafron. Perched on chairs or less luxuriously seated on benches, they yell at Guignol to watch out for the thief, root for him to stand up to his enemies, and reply to questions with joyful cries of "Yes!" or "No!" And when they pour out of the theater of the Champ-de-Mars (a miniature Folies-Bergère), the tiny corral exposed to winter winds and summer sun on the Champs-Élysées (once frequented by Marcel Proust) or one of the vintage theaters of Buttes-Chaumont, they are full of energy, giddy with delight, and satisfied that wrongs have been righted... in short: happy!

Théâtre du Luxembourg
Jardin du Luxembourg, 6th arr.
Tel. 01 43 29 50 97

Les Marionnettes du Champ-de-Mars
Avenue du Général-Margueritte, 7th arr.
Tel. 01 48 56 01 44

Théâtre Vrai Guignolet
Rond-point des Champs-Élysées, 8th arr.
Tel. 01 42 45 38 30

Guignol du Parc Montsouris
23, avenue Reille, 14th arr.
Tel. 06 07 77 85 42

Guignol de Paris
Parc des Buttes-Chaumont, 19th arr.
(Entrance in rue Botzaris)
Tel. 06 98 99 66 24

Théâtre Guignol Anatole
Parc des Buttes-Chaumont, 19th arr.
(Entrance opposite the Mairie)
Tel. 01 40 30 97 60

SEANCES

MERCREDI
à 16H et 17H

SAMEDI
à 16H et 17H

DIMANCHE
à 11H, 16H et 17H

LOST TRADES

> *But the engineers came, and the Cour des Miracles thieves' kitchen was expropriated in the public interest. Farewell to the merriment of our squares, farewell to the motley clothing and strange songs. . . I swear to you, worthy sirs of the city council, Paris is bored. It longs for the return of the picturesque.*

Charles Yriarte, *Les Célébrités de la rue*, 1878

Fruit vendor, knife sharpener, dog groomer, traveling musician, china repairer, bread carrier, tinker, flower girl, one-man band, chair-caner, bird charmer, theater barker, rag dealer, grinder, glazer, street singer, boat hirer, feather duster seller, tooth puller, shoeshine boy, leech applier, bear trainer, "guardian angel" (those who escort drunks home for a tip), cigar-butt collector, lamplighter, live-bird catcher and plucker, chair hirer, flea trainer. . .

These street trades all existed at one time or another. Most are a thing of the past, but some have survived—knife grinders and hot chestnut sellers, for instance. Others may return one day.

ECONOMY OF SCALES

Y ou would have to be impossibly old to remember the day when the first weighing machine appeared in the Luxembourg gardens. Installed at the end of the 19th century, it reigned in solitary splendor until 1911, when Etablissements Chameroy secured a permit to add three others.

The firm paid a fee of 50 francs per annum for each machine and customers were charged five *centimes* to weigh themselves. Of course, weighing machines were a common sight in Paris in those days. You would come across them in public gardens, in front of drugstores, and on subway platforms. Some models had more than just a needle on a dial to show your weight: they also dispensed a printed card smaller and thicker than a métro ticket.

Over the years, these weighing machines steadily vanished from the Parisian landscape. Only three are left in the Luxembourg gardens today. They are in varying states of repair, but all have one thing in common: they no longer work. Even so, tourists still mount them to pose for a picture, and the occasional regular visitor stands on a platform in the vague hope that the mechanism will somehow miraculously have repaired itself. Sadly, the machines—which take only francs—no longer weigh anybody.

Weighing machines
Jardin du Luxembourg, 6th arr.
Two stand beside the Saint-Michel entrance and the third near the tennis courts.

MIDWAY MAGIC

ew still remember the carnivals of yesteryear in the Vaugirard, Batignolles, Montmartre, Maison-Blanche, and Invalides districts. Their noisiness and the traffic jams they caused led to their inexorable exile over the second half of the twentieth century. Paris has changed out of all recognition since 1928, when no less than 38 carnivals contributed to the city's moveable feast. The Denfert-Rochereau event (known as the Fête du Lion de Belfort) was without a doubt the most spectacular—and tentacular, winding as it did through the streets to place d'Alésia. For two weeks from the end of September to mid-October, excited crowds milled around its attractions, circus tents, and menageries.

Today, the most engaging Fête is to be found in the Tuileries gardens. The magnificent formal park broadmindedly accommodates a range of very modern, often eye-catching attractions, together with the traditional assortment of vintage rides, bumper cars, shooting galleries, and fishing games. A mouthwatering scent of cotton candy and caramel apples hangs in the air. . .

**Fête foraine
du jardin des Tuileries**
Place de la Concorde, 1st arr.
November to January

Fête de la place de la Bastille
Place de la Bastille, 11th arr.
All year round

Fête à Neu-Neu
Porte de la Muette,
Bois de Boulogne, 16th arr.
August to October

Foire du Trône
Porte Dorée, bois de Vincennes, 12th arr.
April to May

SPRINGS ETERNAL

Tap water is not everyone's cup of tea, varying as it does in hardness and chlorination from one district to the next. Many opt for mineral water, but nagging voices warn us that its plastic bottles are harmful, releasing toxins and scarring the environment with their ecological footprint.

So is there a way for Parisians to quench their thirst in all good conscience? Indeed there is. They need only visit the fontaine Lamartine in the eponymous square. Residents of the neighboring limestone buildings and pilgrims from further afield regularly fill their bottles there. The water springs from one of the last working artesian wells in the capital. Engineering works began in 1855, but it took six years for the borehole to reach the Albien aquifer more than 550 meters underground. The pure, crystalline, millennial water was used to supply the surrounding area and also to fill the lakes and rivers of the Bois de Boulogne.

By the end of the twentieth century, the well was showing its age, gradually silting up and leaking through aging pipes, so restoration work was carried out in 1996. Since then, cognoscenti have returned to draw water from the *fontaine* on a regular basis. Among them are purists who insist on glass bottles, and health buffs keen to benefit from the water's richer than average iron content. Who can forget the advice of classic French comedian Bourvil, playing the part of an improbable stalwart of the Temperance League: "Liquor, no. . . but ferruginous water, yes!"

Fontaine Lamartine	• **And also:**
Square Lamartine, 16th arr.	Place Paul-Verlaine, 13th arr.
	Square de la Madone, 18th arr.

LAUNDRIES OF LEGEND

While your thick quilted ski jacket can safely be entrusted to the local dry cleaner, that wedding or christening dress handed down from one generation to the next, or precious antique linen, are another story. A story that Maison Parfait, élève de Pouyanne, knows better than anyone. Here, damp cloths, hand finishing, shine removal, and specialty ironing are more than just empty promises or futile gestures. The establishment has been a custodian of high tradition since it was founded in 1903. Advantageously located a step away from that temple to fashion the Printemps department store, its deliciously old-fashioned storefront appeals to the passer-by. The elegant wood-paneled interior is just as delightful. May Parfait long continue to work its painstaking wonders, restoring our most cherished garments to all their former glory.

| **Parfait, élève de Pouyanne**
57, boulevard Haussmann, 8th arr.
Tel. 01 42 65 34 23 | • And also:
Maison Germaine Lesèche
11 *bis*, rue de Surène, 8th arr.
Tel. 01 42 65 12 28 | **Blanchisserie Pergolèse**
7, rue Pergolèse, 16th arr.
Tel. 01 45 00 58 35 |

Délustrage
procédé "Diebold"

CUSTODIANS OF COMFORT

Ping! The characteristic clink of a coin tossed into a china saucer informs us that we are in the presence of a formidable lady restroom attendant—a Cerberus of public lavatories who levies tribute from all those who enter her realm. And woe to those incautious souls who find their pockets empty!

Ping! Today, that clink is only to be heard in a few rare places. The arrival of automatic public toilets—coin-operated, then free—not only decimated the *vespasienne* urinal, but also Paris's public lavatories and the staff charged with their care. Even the superb Art Deco lavatories at the Madeleine have fallen into disuse.

Ping! Yes, the last public lavatories charging admission can be counted on the fingers of one hand. Yet nostalgic sightseers can still visit the Jardin des Champs-Élysées and find a charming 1900-vintage wooden "Chalet of Necessities" that boasts a dozen toilets. The comfort station is somewhat dated, but spotless—thanks to the vigilant ministrations of the lady attendant, one of the last survivors of a very Parisian species that seems destined for extinction.

Chalet de nécessités Ambassadeurs	• And also:
Jardin des Champs-Élysées, 8th	**Lavatories at the foot of Sacré-Coeur**
	1, rue Lamarck, 18th

HELLO, ODÉON 8400?

Admirers of Patrick Modiano's novels and their gentle musicality will be familiar with the significant role played by telephone numbers found on a business card, scribbled on a fluttering scrap of paper, or jotted down in a phonebook or mislaid address book. They invariably begin with legendary, now defunct codes:

KLE 77 94 in *Villa triste* (Dismal Villa).

PAS 47 22 in *Livret de famille* (Family Record).

TUR 92 00 in *L'Herbe des nuits* (Night Grass).

We can roughly date the stories from these alphabetic codes, which were in use for a relatively short time: thirty-five years from 1928 to 1963. All denote telephone exchanges and the districts they served. In all, the twenty-five Parisian exchanges routed 112 area codes. AUTeuil, BAGatelle, JASmin, MIRabeau, and TROcadéro numbers, for instance, were connected to the Auteuil exchange on rue Jasmin and rue Henri-Heine in the sixteenth arrondissement. ALMa, BALzac, and ÉLYsées were assigned to the Élysées exchange on rue La Boétie in the eighth arrondissement. Although connoisseurs can still admire the fine industrial architecture of such exchanges in rue du Louvre (Gutenberg) or rue Sorbier (Ménilmontant), the lettered area codes are now a thing of the past. Today,

they are only to be found when we scrape away the paint on old business signs, watch classic black-and-white movies, immerse ourselves in vintage thrillers, or peruse the yellowing ads in antique magazines.

Aficionados can still find old-style telephones with rotary dials, where letters feature beneath the numbers: 2 = ABC, 3 = DEF, 4 = GHI, 5 = JKL, 6 = MNO, 7 = PRS, 8 = TUV, 9 = WXY. To decode all the Parisian numbers with a 014 prefix, they need only examine the three subsequent digits. For example, in numbers beginning with 014326, allocated to subscribers in the fifth and sixth arrondissements, the 326 can immediately be deciphered as DANton… taking us fifty years back in just a second.

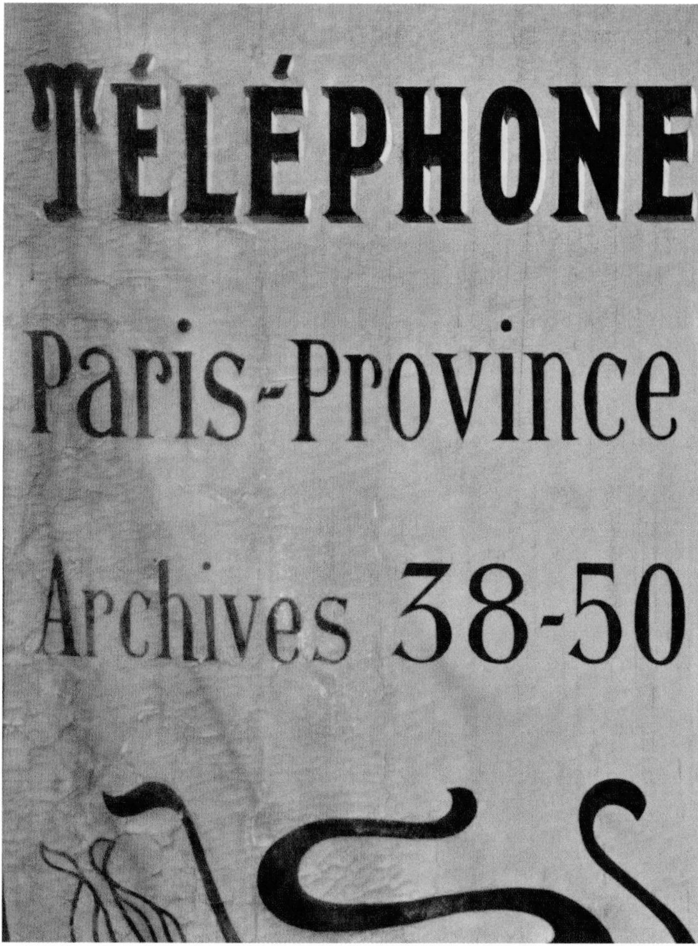
TÉLÉPHONE
Paris-Province
Archives 38-50

NEVERS FOREVER

Behind his red-brick counter with its Seventies yellow plastic sugar dispenser, Rachid serves shots of pastis for two Malian garbage collectors and the English poet who is courteously addressing them in impeccable Franglais: "My wife is French, very pas good la situation dans your pays. . ." Seated at a table that shelters its modesty under a sheet of white paper, a small, solitary gentleman is sampling the contents of his generous, steaming plate of couscous and grinning in delight at this affable entertainment. On the walls, two prints of winter landscapes face each other. Between them looms a large TV, its screen dark at lunchtime, when a little conversation is enough.

Le Nevers is a lively café-restaurant and a hotel, too—its small rooms occupied by sometimes perennial guests (a few have even raised children here). Open since the 1950s, the hostelry still seems to reflect the spirit of that age. Proprietor Rachid came to France almost half a century ago. He has seen the neighborhood change dramatically. Once home to artisans

and petty hoodlums, it was then settled by the Wenzhou community, and is now fast becoming a bastion of "bourgeois Bohemianism." Bracketed by Chinese restaurants, Le Nevers is a miraculous oasis of human warmth, uncaring of social divides and international conflicts. We would cheerfully drop in every day, if only for a coffee at the counter.

Nevers Café-Hôtel
14, rue des Vertus, 3rd arr.
Tel. 01 42 78 08 41

QUAYSIDE CANARIES AND CARNATIONS

To brighten up your day, why not explore this flower market, all too frequently disdained by Parisians? As soon as you emerge from the beautifully preserved Cité Métro station designed by Guimard, its charms are evident. You find yourself in a peaceful, authentic quarter of the Île de la Cité, opposite six 1900s-style glass pavilions brimming with color and fragrance. Floral commerce is a long-established tradition here: these flower sellers have been doing business for almost two hundred years. The aisles are a breath of fresh air, ideal for a relaxing stroll among plants and gardening accessories. Appealing pots of violets in wicker baskets and enameled pitchers from a bygone age delight the visitor. On Sunday, the market plays host to its cousin, a chirpy bird market that draws the crowds. Definitely not for enochlophobes.

Flower Market	**Bird Market**
Place Louis-Lépine and quai de la Corse, 4th arr.	Place Louis-Lépine and quai de la Corse, 4th arr.

IN VINYL VERITAS

Whether they are 15-year-olds in search of vintage Seventies and Eighties sounds to sample, or weathered album-hounds hunting for discs to fill the gaps in their collection, they employ virtually the same technique. The British call it "crate digging," this obsessive urge to rummage through the bins of record dealers, mining for gold.

First, you run your fingertips over a wad of albums (which may or may not be sorted into musical genres or alphabetical order), as though you can sense their content simply by brushing your fingers over the sleeves. Then you lean the records back and the game is afoot! Your thumb and forefinger begin their frantic sprint, flicking forward each vinyl until one suddenly catches your eye. Stop! You take the record out, study the front and back of the sleeve and, if the album passes muster, slip the disc out of its inner sleeve to inspect it. You examine the label, the condition

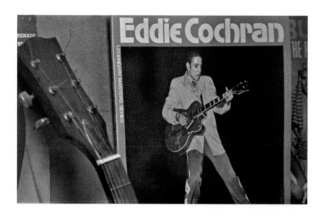

of the grooves, and the die numbers... If the record still meets with your approval, you set it to one side and continue to browse the remaining platters.

Parisian crate-diggers flock to second-hand stores, such as Crocodisc, Boulinier, and LDV, and junk shops, garage sales, and flea markets. Vinyl records began to vanish from most stores 25 years ago, but are still in demand; more than ever, in fact. Sales are steadily rising as CDs decline in popularity. Both younger listeners and more mature music-lovers are rediscovering the incomparable pleasure of handling, listening to, and collecting these delightful LPs... and, of course, talking music with other connoisseurs met by a box in a junk shop.

Crocodisc	**Boulinier**	**Best Ouest**
40, rue des Écoles, 5th arr.	20, boulevard Saint-Michel, 6th arr.	84, rue de l'Ouest, 14th arr.
Tel. 01 43 54 33 22	Tel. 01 43 26 90 57	Tel. 06 88 09 06 13

WILD ABOUT WALTZ

> *Come let's discover those old-fashioned pleasures*
> *Your heart against mine, despite the crazy rhythm*
> *I want to feel your body pressed up close.*
>
> Charles Aznavour, *Les Plaisirs démodés*, 1972

Revived by TV extravaganzas where celebrities whirl acrobatically to the strains of a rumba, cha-cha, or a sultry tango, ballroom dancing's ailing fortunes seem to be on the mend. The genre is gathering a new, extraordinary momentum. The dance floors of Parisian venues teem with nostalgics eager to taste the pleasures of guiding the partner they hold in a firm embrace, with women of character ready for once to yield to the silent commands of a stranger, and with those who are simply keen to share a moment's enjoyment at little (or no) cost. Dancing in pairs and (re)learning the basics of dances that were overshadowed by the disco individualism of the Seventies seem irresistibly attractive.

Elle a appris à danser

Quand il arrive des aventures dans la vie

le fox-trot à de Gaulle

C'est chez Roxy que de Gaulle a appris à danser

« C'était un très bon danseur »

De Gaulle en 1940

Mais il a aussi voulu apprendre le tango

Sur un air de tango, une dame vient de fêter le quarante-neuvième anniversaire du cours de danse qu'elle dirige dans sa ville.

C'est la célèbre Roxy, championne du monde de...

New students are flocking to Georges et Rosy. Here, at one of the top dancing schools in Paris, Charles de Gaulle and Édith Piaf once learned the delights of waltz and foxtrot (but not together!). New pupils are applying every day—some to take the lead on their wedding day or find a soul mate at one of the school's events; others simply for the pleasure of dancing. All these industrious, enthusiastic devotees instill a warm, friendly atmosphere, convinced as they are that dancing is a panacea to cure the solitude of modern existence.

Cours Georges et Rosy
20, rue de Varenne, 7th
Tel. 01 45 48 66 76

BOWLED OVER

A game of French *boules* or *pétanque* is a parenthesis. Time slows to a crawl and the cityscape fades. All eyes are glued to the jack or *cochonnet* and the metal balls, hefted to judge their weight (650 to 800 grams), slowly warmed, and pitched to collide with others in the hope of achieving a *carreau* (positioning shot) or *palet* (ejecting an opponent's ball and leaving yours in its place). As soon as the players lift their *boules*, they are lost to the world and immersed in the tension of the game.

Parisian *pétanqueurs* are young and old, male and female, dilettantes or devotees playing nearly every day. Some are registered members of the FFPJP or another organization, some play for a club and have their own locker, and others compete on an improvised strip of ground after work or during their lunch hour.

Pétanque is not an Olympic event, but it was among the official physical activities and sports of the Universal Exposition of 1900, along with fishing, kite flying, pigeon racing, and—cannon firing!

Union Bouliste du 15e 43, rue Blomet, 15th arr. Tel. 01 45 66 87 21	**Boulodrome du jardin du Luxembourg** Rue Guynemer side, 6th arr.	**Télégraphe bowling grounds** 46, rue du Télégraphe, 20th arr.

WHOLESALE
BACCHANALIA

Long ago, parents and grandparents would set off with their empty bottles to fill them at the local wine merchant's. The wines they bought were not generally of the finest quality, but good enough for everyday consumption. Better vintages were kept for Sundays and special occasions.

At En Vrac (In Bulk) in rue de l'Olive, the casks are back! They are stacked in formation, their spigots dispensing a flow of delightful, reasonably priced red and white wines, chosen from every corner of France. The customers are inevitably delighted. The experience stirs distant memories for the eldest and introduces less seasoned oenophiles to an entertaining, inexpensive, ecological way of buying wine. Already planning their vacation, some head straight for the rosé in a box. Fascinated children eagerly share this special moment with their parents.

Clients bring their own receptacles or ask for the ones supplied by the cellar—stylish copies of vintage lemonade bottles in three sizes: 1 liter, 75 centiliters, and even 50 centiliters for those with more modest thirsts.

The bottles are returnable, of course, as they were all those years ago.

En Vrac	• **And also:**
2, rue de l'Olive, 18th arr.	**Le Baron Bouge**
Tel. 01 53 26 03 94	1, rue Théophile-Roussel, 12th arr.
	Tel. 01 43 43 14 32

BOILED EGGS
ON THE BAR

> *It's compelling, the dull sound of a hard-boiled egg*
> *cracked on a zinc counter. It's compelling, that sound,*
> *when it stirs in the memory of a hungry man.*
>
> Jacques Prévert, from the poem
> *"La grasse matinée"* (The Sleep-In), *Paroles*, 1946

While Prévert undeniably enshrined the hard-boiled egg in our cultural pantheon, the reference may now baffle the younger generation, all because of an administrative order dated May 9, 1995. On that day, the distinctive stands where hard-boiled eggs waited patiently to be chosen were banished from the counters of cafés, bars, and bistros. It was a tough break for the hard-boiled egg.

The reasoning was, of course, based on health and safety. Hard-boiled eggs can be kept in an icebox for up to a week, but at room temperature are soon past their best. Left out too long, a few bad eggs spoiled it for all the others, causing the banishment of the egg stand from Parisian bars.

The days when blue-collar workers setting out early in the morning ate a hard-boiled egg to take the edge off their hunger, washing it down with a coffee (cream and sugar optional), already seem distant. Ladies watching their weight did the same, opting for a breakfast rich in protein and low in calories. For penniless students, eggs were a welcome snack within their limited means.

But those days are gone. . . or almost. Just a few recalcitrant taverns still maintain the tradition of the six-egg stand with its central saltshaker. After the crucial impact of shell on counter edge—not always zinc now— old hands aim to strip away the shell in as few pieces as possible. To each his own technique! The task accomplished, they can savor the egg at their leisure, preceding each bite with a ritual sprinkling of salt.

THE LIVE POETS' SOCIETY

The literary-minded often complain that few people read poetry today, as they see other genres colonizing bookstore shelves formerly devoted to verse. Yet just a stone's throw from Les Invalides, a hospitable group still pays tribute to the canons of Baudelaire, Neruda, Senghor, Laforgue, and Aragon (a friend of Jean-Pierre Rosnay, the society's founder). Once the host of the TV show *Le Club des Poètes*, Rosnay founded this lyrical forum in 1961 and it has changed little over the years. Today, his son Blaise still holds the keys to the theater with its old piano and black-and-white photographs. Their heads filled with rhyming stanzas, habitués of every age step up onto the stage to recite sonnets, odes, and pastorals. Unmoved by fickle fashion, far from the madding crowds, they share their love of fine verse. . . and fine wines, too! "I have taken up the challenge of making poetry infectious and enduring," announced Jean-Pierre Rosnay. Mission accomplished.

Club des Poètes
30, rue de Bourgogne, 7th arr.
Tel. 01 47 05 06 03

WHAT'S THE CATCH?

Parisian anglers are as fascinating to observe as the urban Sunday artists who set up their easels on the sidewalk. Passers-by stop to watch both and sometimes even venture to chat with the happy few, who seem untouched by the ambient roar and bustle of the city.

It is quite easy to fish in Paris, but there are a number of rules governing the sport. First, you will need a fishing permit—issued for a year, a season, or even a day, depending on the level of your ambition. The precious certificate can be obtained over the Internet, but you may prefer to acquire it in a specialty store, where aspiring anglers can purchase the right equipment. For breadth of choice, go to Des Poissons si grands (Such Big Fish), "fishing specialist of the year 2000," in the seventh *arrondissement*. For atmosphere, visit Maison de la Mouche Dubos on the Île Saint-Louis,

a temple founded in the 1930s and now run by a charming octogenarian lady whose expert advice is valued by fly-fishing enthusiasts.

The shop is a miniature paradise for curiosity seekers, too, who will be delighted by its wooden furniture, delicate, colorful flies, and fishing outfits made in France or Scotland, sold here exclusively.

"It's the kind of store you just don't find anymore," its admirers insist.

Once you are suitably equipped, all you have to do is find the right spot to cast your line. Fortunately, the best locations are also the most beautiful. Some swear by the merits of quai de la Tournelle, while others claim that the shores of the Île Saint-Louis teem with carp. In any case, more than catching a few fish, the aim is to enjoy a welcome break by the Seine, alone or in convivial company.

<table>
<tr><td>Des Poissons si grands
160, rue de Grenelle, 7th arr.
and 45, boulevard de La Tour-Maubourg, 7th arr.
Tel. 01 47 53 74 97</td><td>Maison de la Mouche Dubos
1, boulevard Henri-IV, 4th arr.
Tel. 01 43 54 60 46</td></tr>
</table>

SERVICE STATIONS WITH A SMILE

These service stations fronted by vintage pumps (one look and you wonder if they really still work!), with their period enameled advertisements hung on rusty nails, and grimy windows cluttered with cans of oil and antifreeze are very similar to their country cousins, waiting hopefully on sleepy rural lanes. Whichever you visit, you never touch the pump yourself. Service is included— usually with a smile.

But for how long? Neglected by most, these little family businesses could soon be consigned to an unlamented oblivion.

Old-style service stations

5, boulevard Henri-IV, 4th arr.
Tel. 01 43 54 55 64

46, rue des Archives, 4th arr.
Tel. 01 42 72 21 74

40, rue Gay-Lussac, 5th arr.
Tel. 01 43 29 62 02

82, boulevard Saint-Michel, 6th arr.
Tel. 01 43 54 01 79

15, boulevard des Invalides, 7th arr.
Tel. 01 45 51 54 40

13, boulevard de Clichy, 9th arr.
Tel. 01 45 26 13 84

25, boulevard de la Chapelle, 10th arr.
Tel. 01 46 07 95 87

159, quai de Valmy, 10th arr.
Tel. 01 40 34 56 94

THAT OLD CHESTNUT!

As legend, history, or a poetic blend of the two would have it, the chestnut tree left Constantinople in the sixteenth century to put down roots in Paris. Marie de Médici is said to have been fond of the tree, which has since become the favored sentinel of the city's sidewalks. Chestnuts are less popular in gardens, where their thick foliage tends to cast a pall on their reputation. As the popular saying goes, "The chestnut tree's shadow, a gardener's woe, no need for the hoe, it's useless to sow."

And the fruit of the chestnut? In September, children hurry to gather windfalls still encased in their bristling burs. They stuff them into their coats, compete to see who can throw them the farthest, and take them home to carve or paint.

Grownups of every age join in, too. You frequently see an adult crouching to pick up a chestnut. They carefully examine their find, turning it pensively in their hand before tossing it away wistfully or slipping it into a pocket. Do they believe the traditional claim that the fruit can

prevent rheumatism? France's most famous proponent of chestnut therapy is certainly the cultural TV presenter Bernard Pivot, who has carried a chestnut on him for years.

Back in the day, our elders even slipped a chestnut under their pillow when they turned in. Carefully chosen for its roundness, the fruit was supposed to ensure a good night's sleep and keep spirits and phantoms at bay. And Paris has more than its share of spirits and phantoms. A word to the wise. . .

TRUCK OR TREAT?

Although the idea of banning delivery trucks in Paris is regularly discussed, Léon —one of the last truck stops in Paris—is still in business. Opened in the 1920s (its design includes certain Art Deco features), the bistro became the headquarters of the Truck Drivers Defense Union in 1934, when semi-trailers rolled freely down the capital's boulevards.

Yellow Formica, red and white checkered cloths, handwritten menus slipped into plastic folders, wooden chairs, and napkin lockers: all these deliciously outdated curiosities are still to be found at Léon, named for one of its first proprietors. The vintage paradise—a blue-collar enclave in a business district—is still a family business.

It belongs to the Granges (Christian, the father, in the kitchen, and his wife Colette, sister Catherine, and son Rémi all waiting table or officiating behind the counter). The atmosphere is good-humored and the place packed. Staff from the nearby major department stores mingles with white-collar workers from local banks, students from the Lycée Condorcet, and fans of home cooking at knockdown prices, often seated at the same table.

Léon
5, rue de l'Isly, 8th arr.
Tel. 01 43 87 42 77

Sandwiches
Variés

	PRIX EURO
JAMBON cuit___	3,40
PATÉ au choix__	3,40
RILLETTES _____	3,40
SAUCISSON sec__	3,40
SAUCISSON à l'ail	3,40
FROMAGES au choix	3,40

avec BEURRE suppl⁺

Sandwich misète___	3,80
Jambon et Fromage___	3,80
Croissant ou tartine___	1,20

ARCHIPE

THEATRE MUSIQUE ET CINEM

NINI

Sandra Gab

suis top !

Madeleine

Blandine Métayer

Lola

DARWIN

CAV

PHIL

Origin

LES ENFARINES

Comédie explosive